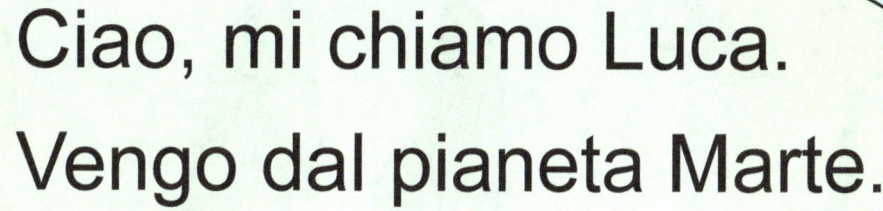

Quando fa caldo

indosso

 una maglietta

e

dei calzoncini.

Quando fa freddo

indosso

 dei pantaloni,

 un maglione

e

 un cappotto.

Quando piove

uso un ombrello.

Quando vado a una festa

indosso

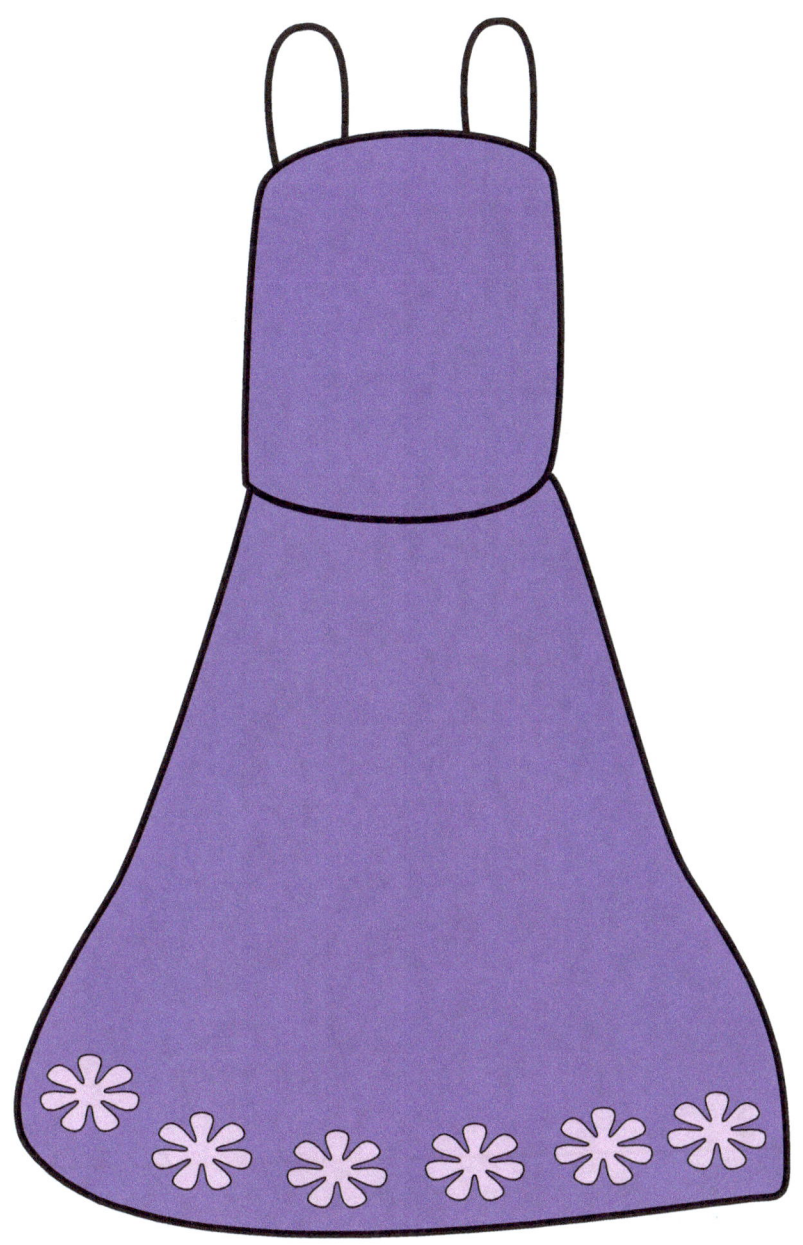

un vestito.

Quando vado al parco

indosso

una maglietta

e

dei jeans.

Quando c'è musica

Quando ho un pallone

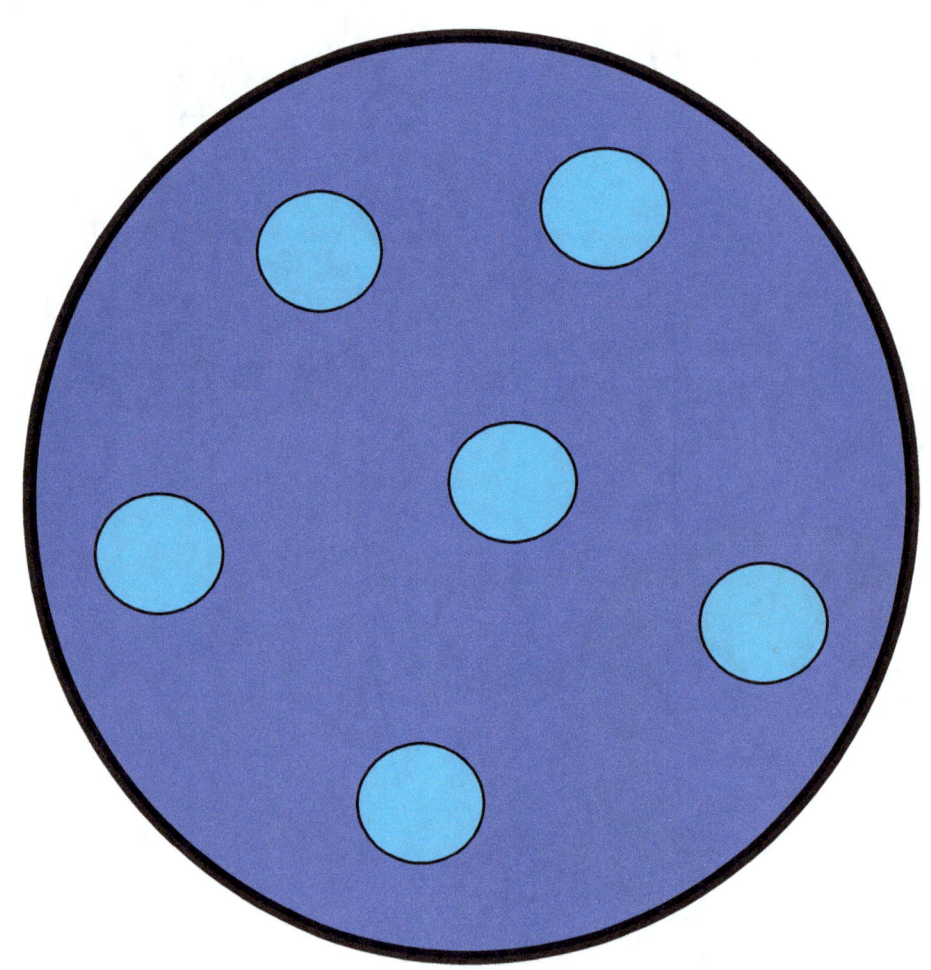

gioco a calcio.

Nella valigia c'è .....

 frutta

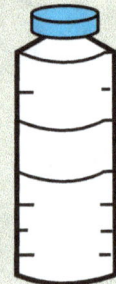 acqua

 musica

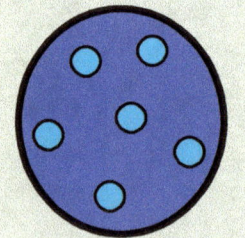 un pallone

 un ombrello

 una maglietta

 un maglione

 dei jeans

 un vestito

 dei pantaloni

 dei calzoncini

 un capotto

I hope you have enjoyed this story! Try to look back at the Italian words from time to time to help you remember them. Reviews help other readers discover my books so please consider leaving a short review on the site where the book was purchased. Your feedback is important to me. Thank you! And have fun learning Italian! It's a lovely language to learn! Joanne Leyland

© Copyright Joanne Leyland 1st edition 2016 2nd edition 2018 3rd edition 2019 4th edition 2021
The useful Italian words and phrases, the song lyrics and the translation of the story may be photocopied for use by the purchasing individual or institution for use in class or at home. The rest of the book may not be photocopied or reproduced digitally without the prior written agreement of the author.

Useful Italian words and phrases

a coat  un capotto	a dress  un vestito	a jumper  un maglione	an umbrella  un ombrello
a t-shirt  una maglietta	jeans 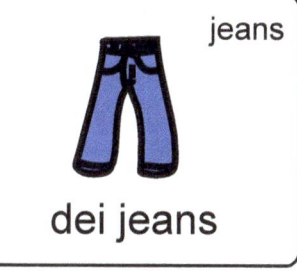 dei jeans	trousers  dei pantaloni	shorts  dei calzoncini
fruit  frutta	water 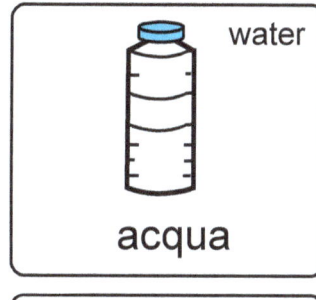 acqua	music  musica	a ball 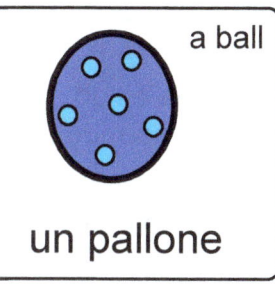 un pallone
the park  il parco	a party  una festa	the suitcase  la valigia	the spaceship 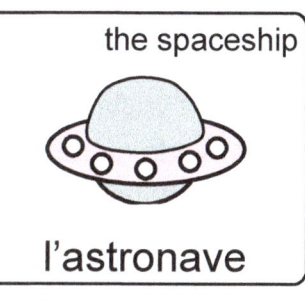 l'astronave

Quando …. When

it's raining  piove	it's cold  fa freddo	it's hot  fa caldo	ho sete — I'm thirsty
			bevo acqua — I drink water
I sing 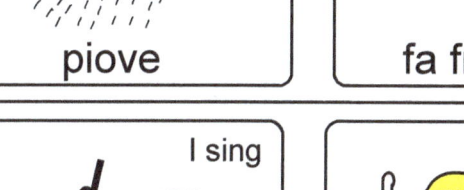 canto	I dance  ballo	I play football  gioco a calcio	ho fame — I'm hungry
			mangio frutta — I eat fruit

© Copyright Joanne Leyland - This page may be photocopied by the purchasing individual or institution for use in class or at home

Italian	English
Ciao, mi chiamo Luca.	Hello, my name is Luke.
Vengo dal pianeta Marte.	I'm from the planet Mars.
Ciao, mi chiamo Anna Maria.	Hello, my name is Anna Maria.
Sono di Roma.	I'm from Rome.
un ombrello	an umbrella
un capotto	a coat
una maglietta	a t-shirt
dei pantaloni	some trousers
un vestito	a dress
dei calzoncini	some shorts
dei jeans	some jeans
un maglione	a jumper
acqua	water
un pallone	a ball
musica	music
frutta	fruit
Perché hai tutte queste cose?	Why do you have all these things?
Non lo capisco!	I don't understand!
Quando fa caldo	When It's hot
indosso una maglietta e dei calzoncini.	I wear a t-shirt and shorts.
Quando fa freddo	When it's cold
indosso dei pantaloni, un maglione e un cappotto.	I wear trousers, a jumper and a coat.
Quando piove	When it rains
uso un ombrello.	I use an umbrella.
Quando vado a una festa	When I go to a party
indosso un vestito.	I wear a dress.
Quando vado al parco	When I go to the park
indosso una maglietta e dei jeans.	I wear a t-shirt and jeans.
Quando ho fame	When I'm hungry
mangio frutta.	I eat some fruit.
Quando ho sete	When I'm thirsty
bevo acqua.	I drink water.
Quando c'è musica	When there's music
canto e ballo.	I sing and I dance.
Quando ho un pallone	When I've a ball
gioco a calcio.	I play football.
Mi piace giocare a calcio.	I like playing football.
Mi piace la tua astronave.	I like your spaceship
È molto grande. È fantastica.	It's very big. It's fantastic.
Mi piace il tuo pianeta.	I like your planet.
Cosa c'è nella valigia?	What's in the suitcase?
Nella valigia c'è …..	In the suitcase there is…
Che buona idea!	What a good idea!
Grazie. Arrivederci! Arrivederci!	Thank you. Goodbye! Goodbye!

© **Joanne Leyland**   1st edition 2016   2nd edition 2018   3rd edition 2019   4th edition 2021

The vocabulary page, the song lyrics and the translation may be photocopied for use by the purchasing individual or institution for use in class or at home. The rest of the book may not be photocopied or reproduced digitally without the prior written agreement of the author.

Let's sing a song!

The following words could either be sung to a made up tune, or you could try saying the words as a rap.

For inspiration of a melody to use you could hum first a nursery rhyme. How many different versions can you create using the lyrics?

Quando piove, quando piove
Uso un ombrello, uso un ombrello
Quando piove, quando piove
Uso un ombrello, uso un ombrello

Quando fa freddo, quando fa freddo
Indosso un cappotto, indosso un cappotto
Quando fa freddo, quando fa freddo
Indosso un cappotto, indosso un cappotto

Quando ho fame, quando ho fame
Mangio frutta, mangio frutta
Quando ho fame, quando ho fame
Mangio frutta, mangio frutta

Quando ho sete, quando ho sete
Bevo acqua, bevo acqua
Quando ho sete, quando ho sete
Bevo acqua, bevo acqua

Quando = when   piove = it rains   uso un ombrello = I use an umbrella

Quando = when   fa freddo = it's cold   indosso un cappotto = I wear a coat

Quando = when   ho fame = I'm hungry   mangio frutta = I eat fruit

Quando = when   ho sete = I'm thirsty   bevo acqua = I drink water

© Copyright Joanne Leyland - This page may be photocopied by the purchasing individual or institution for use in class or at home

For children aged 7-11 there are also the following books by Joanne Leyland:

La Scimmia Che Cambia Colore

A monkey changes colour when he eats something of a different colour. Will he ever return to his usual colour? **Topics**: General conversation, days, colours, food, opinions.

Hai Un Animale Domestico?

Marco doesn't have a pet. Will his wish for a pet come true?
Topics: Types of pets, colours, sizes, names of pets, opinions.

Italian Word Games

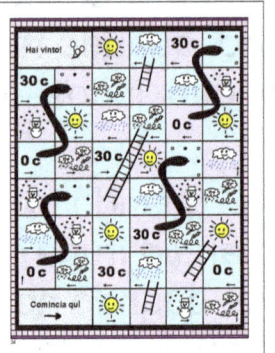

Have fun learning Italian whilst playing games! The 15 topics include the house, the town, the summer, the family, the farm, fruit, ice creams, winter, sea, the restaurant, the supermarket …

First 100 Words In Italian Coloring Book Cool Kids Speak Italian

The 100 Italian words include food, animals, transport, toys, clothes, a fairy, a dinosaur, a mermaid, a dragon etc. The 30 delightful pages all have borders and are single sided.

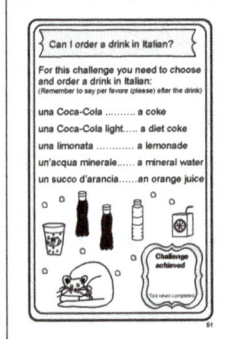

On Holiday In Italy Cool Kids Speak Italian

Designed especially to teach Italian to children who are going on holiday, and then to challenge them to speak Italian whilst away.

Topics include: Greetings, Essential words, Numbers, Drinks, Italian food, Ice creams, Hotels, Campsites & Around town.

For more information about learning Italian and the great books by Joanne Leyland go to https://funitalianforkids.com